Ox

MARTIN HAYES

ILLUSTRATED BY
GUSTAVIUS PAYNE

KFS

Newton-le-Willows

Published in the United Kingdom in 2021
by The Knives Forks And Spoons Press,
51 Pipit Avenue,
Newton-le-Willows,
Merseyside,
WA12 9RG.

ISBN 978-1-912211-81-4

Supported using public funding by
ARTS COUNCIL
ENGLAND
LOTTERY FUNDED

For Stella Wulf – who knows her Cows from her Oxen

Contents

Ox

Martin Hayes

How Moos Replaced Roars

(after receiving a final letter of warning from Farmer for writing words up
on the leaky barn wall that he thought brought the farm into disrepute)

due to the adverse publicity
of recently getting caught
chucking words out into the corner of a vast canyon
millions of miles from the centre
of anything that actually matters
Ox has realised that he is just an ox
and not a farmer

Ox has realised
that he isn't supposed to have dreams
or an opinion
anymore

it has taken a few weeks for Ox to adjust
to start feeling like an ox again
but now that he has it under control

he loves arching his back up under the moon
while letting out deep and low moos

he loves refusing to lay down on the ground
15 minutes every time before it rains

he loves refusing to budge from his leaky barn
when it is time to file out into the yard
so that he can be strapped into one of their ploughs

and he loves
remembering the old songs
about when oxen were allowed to be oxen
and not have to mind every moo or fart
that exited from them

in fact
thinking about it
being an ox
could be very much like before
when Ox was just a pair of hooves
making as much money as possible
for Farmer

only the leftover angry hoofprints in the rain-trodden grass
will have to be more disguised
and the anger
will have to sound more like an ox mooing out from a leaky barn
rather than roars
heard from a distant part of the jungle

Martin Hayes

Ox's Descent

when Ox was born
it was like a rotten tooth falling out of an old ulcerated mouth

when Ox mooed his first moo
it was like a whisper spoken into a cupped hand
in the furthest corner of the steepest widest canyon
of Earth

when Ox got to his feet
and took his first step
it was like a car losing control on an isolated road
miles up in the mountains

when Ox got strapped into his first plough
it was like a revelation
only with mud and hunger and fear

and when Ox realised
this was it
that all of the centuries
had funnelled their way to this point
to this X on the map
with him now standing on it
wracked with anxiety and sweat
it felt like being in a nest full of starlings
with a stoat's head
appearing over its edge every three seconds
like on a time loop

if nothing else
Ox was now ready
for life on the farm

Martin Hayes

Ox Gets Sized Up

the never ending flanks of rippling muscle needy to be put to work

the depths to the eyes filled with nothing upon nothing

the vein's openness wide as a motorway letting all of that blood thunder through

the scrotum big as a sack of space hoppers containing all of those slaves

the mind simple as a puppy in a pen four times more gullible

and that great big stupid heart of his
size of Fox
marauding about inside his chest
unable to sleep
unable to relax
needing to do

hmm – Farmer thought to himself
as The Idea flashed through his mind
these are just the blocks I need
to build me a farm with

Martin Hayes

Ox and the Bottom Line
Is All That Counts Method

down on the farm
Farmer is counting the cost
of having so many oxen
he adds up columns of figures
moves columns around
places some of the figures from one column
into another column
but no matter how hard Farmer tries
he cannot work out how he can make
even more money
he just has too many oxen to pay for

so Farmer has an idea
if he can establish
using the bottom line is all that counts method
placed against the cost involved
in keeping each individual ox
then maybe he can arrive at a formula
which he can use to decide which ox
can be sent off to be slaughtered
and save a little bit of money

after all
saving is exactly the same thing as making
on a farm

again he does all the math
dividing acres by hours by the speed at which oxen are known
to pull a plough
but nothing obvious jumps out at him

Farmer is resilient though
he knows he can't just go around slaughtering oxen
so that he can make even more money
he knows that there needs to be a just and reasonable process
that can be defined in a court of law
before any ox can even be touched
never mind slaughtered

so he begins working out how many days off each ox has
due to coughing
or lungworm
or cryptosporidium
cross-referencing the results
against which oxen eat more hay
or which oxen demand more of his attention
to be looked after
trying to separate one ox from another ox
to see if he can justify
its slaughter

if nothing else
slaughtering one ox will show all the other oxen
that Farmer means business
that they'd all better start pulling his bloody ploughs harder
if only to cover for their slaughtered colleague
if only to justify
their still beating hearts

unfortunately
Farmer concludes
he does need all of his oxen
or more to the point
he does need all of them pulling his ploughs
because that's what keeps the farm ticking
and making him money
it's just that he doesn't need
all of these damn fucking oxen

Martin Hayes

Ox Hunger

the oxen have noticed
that over the years
they were being given smaller and smaller amounts of food
by Farmer

it's got so bad lately
that when they sit down to eat
they are never able to remove
the hunger from their guts
or work out why
this has been allowed to happen to them

out in the fields
on a particularly harsh winter's day
one of the oxen perished
while pulling its plough

Farmer quickly had the ox removed
but all of the oxen saw it or heard about it
and it wasn't long before they were all talking amongst themselves

after much debate and rumour
it was decided that the ox had died
because it wasn't being given enough food
to sustain it while doing its job
that any one of the other oxen
could be next
if they didn't do something about it

being oxen it wasn't easy to arrive on a strategy
they all agreed upon
so in the end

the best they could come up with
was to write Farmer a letter
telling him how hungry they were
how unfair it was
giving them these tiny amounts of food
when Farmer and his family had so much to eat at each sitting
they could chuck food away
as though it grew on trees

after reading the letter
Farmer couldn't help but agree
it did seem unfair
especially considering
that nothing was going to change
in this lifetime
or the next one

Martin Hayes

Ox Staring off into Space

after the oxen had finished their day's toil out in the fields
they were herded back into their leaky barns
where they would be expected to eat their paltry amounts of food
then just lay there
or stand around
swishing their tails

it got so boring
that though the oxen didn't often speak to each other
there were some times
when it just became unavoidable

and then they would talk about the weather or Farmer's thwacking stick
or about buttercups and storms
but once the conversation got going
it quickly came to an end

then after having used up all of their words
they would just stare
boss-eyed
three inches out in front of them

and that's when
one of the oxen would inevitably ask
out of embarrassment or nervousness
that same old question

so what is it with Farmer
always singing about that Lord of his
how plentiful and rich
He has made his life?
I mean
we haven't got a Lord to sing about
have we?

none of the oxen knew if this was a rhetorical question
or directed at them
but they knew that it was a true statement

as they all twitched their noses
letting their eyes bulge a little bit larger
staring off past the stars into space
knowing whatever it was that was out there
it sure looked cold and hungry

Martin Hayes

Ox and the Struggle Against the Single File Entry Method

when Ox felt ill
and couldn't face filing out into the yard
along with the other oxen
so that they could all be strapped into their ploughs
Farmer came into the leaky barn
and just stood there
in front of him
and said

so what's the matter with you today
Ox?

the ox mooed
deep and low
but Farmer didn't understand
because farmers don't understand
deep and low moos
they only understand the single file entry method
into the straps of their ploughs

so Farmer put his elbow-length gloves on
and stuck an arm up Ox's arse
feeling about
for anything that might disprove
how ill Ox said he felt

let's see what's up here then

Farmer said

---

then he pulled at what was inside
he pinched at what was inside
he tweaked and tried to part
what was inside
and when he couldn't find anything
he yanked at the only thing he could get hold of
which was Ox's guts

and because farmers think
that an oxen's guts
are full of shit
Farmer pronounced

there is nothing wrong with you
you are faking it
you are full of shit
and you will not eat tonight

then he twisted a black mark into Ox's forehead
with his thumb

and Farmer was true to his word
withholding Ox's food
so that Ox remained hungry
letting out moos
deep and low

Martin Hayes

Ox Experience

Ox was never going to understand
Einstein's general theory of relativity
what Schrodinger's cat meant
or that tears contain salt
because they come from pain
but you could bet your very last pound
that every ox out there in the fields
or sat inside their leaky barns
after their 11-hour shifts had finished
totally understood and grasped
both theoretically and practically
what a hard day's graft
doesn't get you

Martin Hayes

Ox Dreams About the Siege of Troy

Not me the General
Not me Agamemnon
Not me the demi-god ankle-winged
rising up above the melee to impart my wisdom

Not me in a chariot
lopping off heads with a flame-thrower of a sword
Not me in a tent
reclining on a chaise longue after battle
eating golden apples from a golden dish
having my shoulders rubbed
by female me's
Not me the glory Not me the spoils

just me dying
me dying here me dying there
them over there? me
dying
me dying in rivers
me dying in ditches
me dying with spears thrust into my chest
me crawling around through mud
with everything below my hips
missing
me with my head torn open
hit by a shell made by me in a factory
that's going to close one day
and leave me starving
me homeless

me losing our blood me losing our minds
trying to take a city
for an Idea
that one day will be covered over by sand
never to be found again

Ox suddenly woke up
looking around the leaky barn
he felt terrified
as every other ox seemed to be anesthetized
sleeping and dreaming away about the pointless struggles
Farmer had infected them with

Martin Hayes

Ox in Front of Mirror Mirror on the Wall

I am the biggest creature that walks the surface of this Earth

You're not actually – Elephant is

I am the strongest creature that walks the surface of this Earth

No – that'd be Elephant too

More creatures are in fear of me
than any other creature that walks the surface of this Earth

Nope – that'd be Farmer

I am the most revered creature that walks

Err – don't think so – Lion and Orangutan are far more revered than you

I am the greatest creature that walks

No you're not – Worm is far greater than you
it walks and survives in oh so many ways
that you have yet to learn

I am the first creature to be made in the image of Him

That's debatable and very unlikely

I am beautiful

Well that's subjective for most you are merely a herd animal
with no guts to speak of at all

I am a creature

Yes – you are certainly that

I am

We all are

I …

but before he could finish
the blizzard came in from the hills
sweeping the field up into a whiteout
as Ox stood there shivering
not sure of what to ask next
because every thing had already fled
forgetting him entirely

Martin Hayes

Ox and the Great Big Identity Trick

Ox wants more food in his bowl
he wants the hours he spends strapped into Farmer's plough
reduced

Hen wants to lay her eggs
au naturel
not forced out of her
by a billion-pound industry
that keeps mucking around with the light

Raven wants to hunt Worm
sitting in a tree of an early morning squawking up at the sun
coaxing the blues out of her black back
rather than having to stand on a slagheap
pecking through plastic to get at the proteins and fat
she needs to carry on her struggle

Pig doesn't want to be boxed into a shed and fed pellets
that bloats and makes her develop fat deposits
in places she doesn't want
she wants to be left alone
to snort and rummage through the scrub
until she becomes naturally fat
for slaughter

that she can handle

Cow wants to fall in love with Ox
her milk to be a secret
only shared with her offspring
not to be artificially inseminated
by any old oxen's sperm
over and over again
so that all she has become
in some eyes
is a walking barrel of milk

Kestrel wants to glide
high up in the blue and everlasting
looking for things he can push back his wings at
then nosedive
not this dome of dead dreams and boiling clouds
filled with the acid of one-eyed men
who think they are king

Hare doesn't care
Hare just darts about
here and then there
running as fast as he can
hoping that nothing will catch him
like it seems to have caught everyone else

every animal on the farm
wants what they want
as Farmer sits in the safety of his farmhouse
laughing away at his luck
as not only does God obviously love him
but it seems that all the animals
have fallen for The Great Big Identity Trick
become so wrapped up in themselves
that they'll never get together now
to burn his farmhouse down

Martin Hayes

Ox Writes a Contract

give me a field
and I will give you 11-hours of my sweat

give me a wall
and I will show you how to shoulder it
down

give me a war
and I will bring to you an army of us

give me big bowls of food
and I will let you sit on my back

give me a roof over my head
solid
and I will bring you bigger armies bigger shoulders

give me love
and I will show you what an ox is made of

withhold any of the above
lines will be drawn in the sand
in blood

the contract was drawn up on paper
Ox
thought it sounded fair
and the rest of the herd
agreed
this is how it should be

but upon presentation to Farmer
he said once again that there were more clauses to insert
screwed it up into a ball
threw it on the fire
and continued sipping at his glass of whisky

this has been going on for so long now
not even Owl can remember
who started it all off first

Martin Hayes

Ox Becomes a Possible Threat

while God made paper airplanes out of the flesh of his failed creations
Ox was eating grass – farting – eating grass

while God pulled dinosaurs out of his overworked brain
Ox was in the fields
hunting buttercups
pretending to be a gladiator

while God finger-swirled the rings around Saturn
Ox let 4lbs of shit fall from between his buttocks
walked off

while God handed over his dominion to the first Pope
Ox farted again

while God watched his congregation diminish
Ox watched his numbers grow

God thought
there is something going on here
that I'm not in control of

and that's why
He invented Farmer

Ox and Farmer in God's Trap

every Sunday around mid-morning
Farmer takes his family to church
leaving the oxen untethered
in the holding field behind the farmhouse

and as Farmer is thanking God
for his good luck and riches
so the oxen are also looking up into the sky
or deep deep within them
thanking God for taking Farmer
and his incessant brutal laws
away from the farm
even if it was only for half a day
every Sunday

and so God establishes his kingdom on Earth

purely because the good luck and riches
the food
and the little bits of peace
must come from somewhere

you've got to take your hat off to the Fella
if someone isn't thanking him
for giving
then someone else is thanking him
for taking away

Martin Hayes

Ox Gets Swindled Again

the relationship with the fields was indecipherable
God's hands worked the trees like a glove-puppet
they opened up the skies
made the rivers overrun
the rain keep coming
throwing down the lightning
all it of it beginning and ending
in mud

everything stuck
like bird-song in Ox's mind
until dreams misted his eyes
to see only more dreams

the pain was not a lance in the side
a bolt through the head
but those dreams he dreamt
beautifully rendered vividly coloured
like you could reach out to them
and touch Hope

while deep down
God's hands worked away furiously
trying to hide the only Absolute creation
the greatest lie
that all there truly is
is mud

Ox and Those Questions

it was good being an ox sometimes
out in the fields
yoked to another ox
with the sun up
the breeze warm as a pair of lovers lips
canoodling with his flanks of muscle

it made him feel content
like when he used to be able to stand in a kitchen
roasting a chicken dinner
for the calves to eat

the problems only started
when Ox began to wonder
what might be on the other side of those hills
rising up at the furthest end of the field

that is when Ox stopped being just an ox
and thought to question
why the harness?
why the regulated hours?
why the total acceptance
of just a little bit of hay
to keep Ox going?
why the pain
the lack of moos
heard?

is this
all that there is?

Martin Hayes

when an ox starts asking those sorts of questions
that's when an ox starts becoming a problem
and why
there is a multi-billion-pound industry
producing thwacking sticks
for farmers to hold

Ox Happening on a Stance

the oxen gathered down in the bottom field
out of sight of the farmhouse
under the most threatening swollen-dark-black silver-tinged-sky
ever

shouldn't we be lying down?

one of the oxen said

no

one of the other oxen said

that is exactly what Farmer will be expecting us to do
we mustn't let ourselves be so easily read
we must
through our individualism and unity
let Farmer know
that we mean business

individualism and unity?
all of the oxen looked at each other confused
and began scratching their heads

brilliant!

the same ox said

we must remember to do exactly that
while out in the fields
when we are pulling his ploughs

Ox and Those Voices

after Farmer needed to get the field ready again
so he could plant more seeds
for gold to grow up out of the earth

after Ox had been working
pulling ploughs across the field for 38-days solid
under the sun
under the wind and the rain
or whatever else decided to come

Ox started to hear voices
inside his head

kill the Farmer

kill the Farmer

no matter how much Ox swished his head about
trying to get them to drop out of his ear
or fall out of his nose
the voices wouldn't budge

kill the Farmer

kill the Farmer

even at night time
when everything else was asleep
and he lay looking at moonlight
casting its spells through the cracks in the leaky barn
still those voices
stamping around inside his head

Martin Hayes

kill the Farmer

kill the Farmer

and when
Farmer decided to buy another field
that would need making ready
need ploughing
so that an even more abundance of gold
could grow up out of the earth
the voices turned themselves up
and started screaming

KILL THE FARMER!

KILL THE FARMER!

but nothing happened
Farmer wasn't killed
or held to account
because farmers are never killed
and very rarely held to account

only Ox
developed a twitch
and a growth on his testicles
which Vet said
was a type of cancer

but he couldn't hear the voices
never mind diagnose
or treat them

so for the rest of his existence
Ox ate his food
and pulled his plough around
to a looped soundtrack screaming out inside his head …

KILL THE FARMER!

KILL THE FARMER!

Ox Trust

the oxen bought tickets to the annual oxen versus goats football match
which though having stellar meaning in the ox and goat world
nevertheless had to be played in a secret location
because oxen and goats are not allowed to play football anymore – silly

none of the goats were as forward thinking as the oxen
who because they were armed with infinitesimally bigger brains
had gone and got themselves a coach

the coach was not an ox
or a goat
but an ex-Farmer
who had fallen foul of The National Bank Of Farmer's interest rates
losing everything

being on hard times
he'd answered an advert in the paper
and after one single clandestine meeting
landed the job
of becoming the oxen's new football coach

he coached at a higher standard
than any goat or ox had ever done
and tactically
he was aeons ahead of all the goats and oxen
who all had clods for brains

all of the oxen were so happy and excited
they felt sure that with the ex-Farmer's help
they were going to inflict the heaviest defeat on the goats
in history

Martin Hayes

on the night before the match
just after the team had been selected
it was revealed to the ex-Farmer
the secret location of tomorrow's match
and as soon as the coast was clear
the ex-Farmer dialled the manager of The National Bank Of Farmers
offering him information
that would make him very important indeed
but only if The National Bank Of Farmers
gave him back
his farm

at the secret location
all the oxen and goats were slaughtered on the spot
and the only evidence
was the following unfinished sentence
scraped into the floor in blood
by what looked like an oxen's hoof

once a farmer
always a far ...

Ox Knew His Place

he knew he'd never become
a Royal Highland Show 5-Star Rosette winner
like he'd dreamed
he knew he'd never be able to visit
the South Downs
or sail the Straits of Malacca
like the Elders did
he knew he'd never get to sit on a beach
without worrying about how he was going to pay for it
he knew deep down
inside his big fatty oxen heart
that all he was
was an ox

it's just he didn't need
the constant thwack of Farmer's thwacking stick
on his rump
against his shoulders
across the back of his head

what was it?
to remind him that he was just an ox?
to let him know where he stood
in the pecking order of the farm?
or was it because Farmer
needed to show how much
he was in control of things?

because if it was that
Ox already knew it
he already knew
that what was on the other side of those hills

Martin Hayes

rising up at the end of the fields
boiling in the early mists
of yet-another-morning
is where dreams lay
opened up like a fairytale
that he'd never get to live in
or
trample over

Ox Gets Bullied

why me?

Ox asked
as Farmer thwacked him across the back
with his thwacking stick

shut up!

Farmer said

*just keep facing forwards
and pulling*

then he thwacked Ox again

why me?

Ox asked again

this is so unfair

*I thought I told you
to shut up*

Farmer said

as he thwacked and thwacked away
across Ox's back

finally
Ox's legs buckled
and he fell to the floor
expecting the thwacks then to come
raining down on his head …

Martin Hayes

but Farmer was already off
heading back to the farmhouse
where he would later sit peacefully
with his wife over dinner
impressing her with the details
of how he kept his great big farm going

Ox and the Apprentice Farmer

when Farmer left the farm for his two-week safari trip to South Africa
the oxen rejoiced merrily inside their leaky barns
thinking that for the next two weeks
they wouldn't have to pull their ploughs as hard
or have to endure the thwack of Farmer's thwacking stick
whenever they stopped momentarily in the fields
so they could remember once again
the stories that Elder Ox now long dead
used to share with them when they were calves –
about the land of deathless peace
where oxen were allowed to be oxen
sauntering around fields hunting buttercups
where the only thing that was expected of them
was to lay down 15 minutes
every time before it rained

unfortunately the oxen were once again mistaken

Farmer had given his thwacking stick to the apprentice farmer
who had promised Farmer that when he came back
every square-inch of the fields
would have been ploughed
and not only that
but he would show Farmer
that he could make those oxen work
like not even Farmer could
and still save on the costs of their food

and so it came to pass
until Farmer returned from South Africa
needing a new thwacking stick
because the old one had been broken over an ox's back
and four fewer oxen to feed
because their starved carcasses

Martin Hayes

lay under a tarpaulin sheet
beside the leaky barn

apprentice farmers
because they don't have to absorb the costs or care
about the thwacking and the blood and the death
are notoriously known to treat oxen worse
than Farmer

Ox Begins to Give Up

when Ox knew that he had made it as far as he could
that crossing the hills at the far end of the field
where the fairy tales live
was just a pipe dream
he sat back in his leaky barn
wedged up against a bale of hay
smoking a cheap cigar
laughing

no one can threaten me anymore

I am slave of oxen
I am prisoner of the fields
I am victim of all I survey

he thought to himself

the other oxen looked at him
over their tiny bowls of food
wondering how he could look so content
when all they felt
was the long day's graft
tearing away at their lungs their muscles their minds

how come you can come back
after 11-hours in the field
and look so happy
when the rest of us
can never get rid of the pain?

Ox took a deep drag on his cigar
puffed a cloud of smoke into the air
and said

Martin Hayes

listen mate we are oxen
always have always will be
oxen make things happen
for Farmer only
so there's no need to worry
no need to get anxious
you just gotta give in
we work and eat when we're allowed
and then we don't
so relax brother
put your dreams away
and make the most of it
there's nothin you can do about nothin

Ox took another puff on his cigar
filling the barn up with smoke
as outside
Farmer turned away from the crack in the barn
his face suddenly lit up by sunlight
letting the biggest smile ever seen
spread across his face

Ox at the Bus Stop

as Ox stands at the gate
strapped into his plough
ready to go out and earn

the sun is a flamethrower
directing molten light into his eyes

the wind is a cattail whip
lashing its knuckles
into his before and ever after

behind the hills off in the distance
were the plots of fairy tales
that he'd never get to play a part in

and when the bell rang
signalling his journey was about to start
the field in front of him
was the Somme
about to drink his blood

Ypres
with the lungs of his dead brothers
fossilising in the mud
yellow as mustard

and at around 5 pm
Ox would be called back
returned to the leaky barn
tired as the end of a marriage

unable to moo

Martin Hayes

unable to love

unable to think
of anything
other than
when will the end to all of this
be written

Ox Confronting Technology

when the tractors were unveiled
the oxen knew that their time was up
that it wouldn't be long
before Farmer wouldn't have to feed them anymore
so would be able to justify
sending them for slaughter

this caused a lot of panic and distress in the herd
but some of the brighter oxen said

hold on a minute
there's no need to panic
these tractors don't drive themselves you know
there's an obvious opportunity here
that we're just not seeing

so these forward thinking oxen
applied for the jobs
to drive the tractors
over the fields

at the theory part of the interview
they stated their case

no one knows these fields like we do
we have trodden and heaved your ploughs
over every square-inch of these fields
for years
we are the best and most equipped
for the job

Martin Hayes

Farmer had to agree
they had indeed trodden and heaved his ploughs
over every square-inch of the fields
and no one knew them like they did
all that was left to do
was to see if they could drive the tractors

obviously this didn't go so well
even though they knew which way to steer them
they had trouble getting themselves up on the seats
and their hooves couldn't grip the steering wheels
and when the tractor engines roared into life
they thought that the end of the world was coming
and bolted
knocking Farmer over
running around like lunatics
smashing their heads into walls and gates
before falling unconscious
in puddles of mud

needless to say
they didn't get the job
and now they lay in their leaky barns
nursing headaches
                    ashamed
and redundant

Martin Hayes

Ox Spying the Future

the oxen saw the tractors arrive
in two big articulated trucks
they were loaded off by fork-lift
and quickly stored in the secret barn
behind Farmer's house

it spread like wild-fire around the herd
causing panic and distress
and some of the oxen
to remember what Elder Ox now long dead
had said

there will come a day
when ox will not be needed
anymore to pull the ploughs
when ox will be nothing more
than part of exhibitions
in Farmer's museums

well that day had come

and the oxen mooed out in panic

and the oxen mooed out in distress

and a big rolling voice
came from under the mountains
and spread across the land
not unlike thunder
saying

now that the oxen are done for
let's get to work on the farmers

Ox at Pompeii

there was muscle there was music there was the dark mosaic in the eyes
reflecting the liquefied plains the scorched skirts of the mountain
rooted to the end of something else

God's boredom? God's isolated cruelty?

there was saliva also – so much saliva
crusted around everything
caked like a salt preserving a scream

nothing moved in this sudden absence of movement

the Universe stood still as Ox arched his back
and was caught
in the moment everything erupted
in flash-bulb lava
only to be placed in the museum
as Lot 3031

Martin Hayes

Ox Doesn't Understand Time

the oxen didn't understand time like Farmer did

every situation they found themselves in
was the last one

every time the plough was tightened into their backs
this was it
for eternity

every time they were herded back into their leaky barns
after their shifts in the fields had finished
this aching and numbness
was never going to stop

and every time their stomachs rumbled with hunger
they were all going to starve

Farmer on the other hand
knew about time
he knew that after a hard day's graft
marshalling his oxen out in the fields
all it would take
was a hearty meal
a long hot soak
and a good night's sleep
before he would be ready to go out
and do it all over again tomorrow

but the biggest advantage Farmer had over the oxen
was the knowledge that after fourteen more summers
he would have enough stored up inside the oak tree
to sell the farm
and move to South Africa
where he planned to hunt game
and wear a big Stetson hat

while the oxen knew so little about time
they couldn't see past the moment
they couldn't see past the pain
they couldn't see past the hunger
always running around mooing about their lot
about how it will never change
because for oxen
it never does

this is why oxen quickly learn to forget about dreams
and why farmers
sit in their tractors all day
dreaming and whistling away
until enough summers have passed
for winter to bring along
its big Stetson hat

Martin Hayes

Ox in the Gig Economy

once upon a time
a very long time ago
all the oxen in all the world
were self-employed

they wandered from field to field eating grass
hunting buttercups
whenever they wanted to

but one day
farmers started coming
cordoning off field after field
putting up plaques with their names engraved on them
declaring this piece of land theirs
and that piece of land
theirs

it wasn't long before everywhere
was owned
and the oxen became trapped in fields
they hadn't chosen

every time they walked from one end of a field
to the other end of a field
they found hedges barring their way
only the birds were free
so they gave up in the end
and just stood there
flicking their tails
waiting for what Farmer
was going to do next

it wasn't long before they found out –
Farmer was planning on changing their status
from self-employed

to employed
which meant the oxen would have to do whatever Farmer said
no more sauntering around fields hunting buttercups
or sniffing out storms
it would now just be
grind
grind
grind
until they either became too old
or too sick
to grind anymore

on reflection
though they never really knew
where their next meal was coming from
whether or not they would have a leaky barn to sleep under
or what their little calves would do
if ever they fell sick
being self-employed suited the oxen

it gave them the freedom
to go and hunt in other fields
undetected
to not be banished from fields
they weren't strictly allowed
to eat in

it suited them
much more than this visible 'employed' thingamajig
they now had been lumbered with
where they had to
grind
grind
grind
or else get thwacked with Farmer's thwacking stick
until one day
they either dropped down dead
or else became
superfluous to requirements

Martin Hayes

Ox in Hunger Wonders About His Colleague Mole

the starter
a torn-out tongue
tender with years of grubby language
softening up its muscle

next
the Earth's platter
spread with the scorched heads of its occupants mouths agape
stuck in charred-black laughter
from the high temperatures of a sudden cooking

loosened teeth
to be sucked clean of their leftover gum-flesh
hanging on to their upturned roots
as an ache inherits the mouth of all those that are left

the wine
blood upon blood
deep as the dark of Moles' eyes
after culling

then later
dessert
the cream of white fat opened up at Orgreave beautifully rendered
beaten soft and silky to drip
like victory down their iron throats

the feast is never over never done

Ox's tail still wags within its bones
but he knows it won't be long
before Farmer will work out a way
to snap it open get in there
and lick at the marrow of his insides
too

Ox Exposed to Gloabalisation

first there was 1
then there were 3
then 10
then 15
then before any ox could moo anything about it
there were dozens of new oxen on the farm

it had been rumored that they were coming
but it wasn't until the wall broke down
over on the farthest side of the farm
that Farmer was able
to get them in

the oxen couldn't understand what the new oxen said
their moos sounded different
like they had first been covered in mud
before being let out of their mouths

but what the oxen could see and understand
was that the new oxen really knew
how to pull those ploughs

they pulled and heaved those ploughs
under the sun and through the wind and rain
like their very lives
depended on it

and what's more
when the day was over
and they were all led back into the leaky barn
the new oxen would congregate
up the other end
near the chicken coup
where they would eat their even smaller amounts of food
without moaning or trembling or a voice or
anything

Martin Hayes

as Farmer skipped and danced across the farmyard
thanking the Lord for his luck
as not only did he seem to have come across a new
tougher less organised workforce
but it also looked like it was going to save him
thousands of pounds on hay

Ox in Forced Retirement

though the sun was burning away in the sky
without a cloud to be seen
from horizon to horizon
the oxen lay down in the field
anyway

some oxen still had just about enough energy left
to flick their tails
as flies buzzed and crashed into their rumps
as cows came and went in heat
without any interest from the bulls
and buttercups grew unendangered
for the first time since the Mesozoic period

all together
it was a thoroughly depressing picture

with nothing left to do and nothing expected of them anymore
they had been dumped in the holding field
to await slaughter
or death by hunger
as over the hedge
they could hear the new oxen heaving their ploughs
mooing out together in song

hold on a minute
all of the oxen thought in unison
that song sounds familiar …

no matter how hard we work
we are never given enough
food
no matter how cold we get
we are never given enough
warmth

Martin Hayes

Farmer is an evil monster
who hides behind his
thwacking stick

we want to charge him
we want to trample him
we want to put our hooves
through his head

it made the oxen lament
hearing that song once again
and very very angry
that another group of oxen were singing it
rather than them
as though they hated their old jobs
it was awful having them taken away like that

but it didn't matter
it wasn't as though they could do anything about it

so the two different sets of oxen
passed each other by in history
one lot with jobs
the other lot without them
blaming each other for their unhappy existence
as the sun burned away in the sky
and Farmer
just got richer and richer

Ox Goes to the Poles

all of the oxen were unhappy
always mooing about their lot
work work work
toil toil toil
the sun wasn't as warm as they'd been taught
winter was colder than they could ever remember
food was always 11-hours out in the fields away
always underwhelming
never enough

the noise they made could be heard right the way down through the valleys
it rose up above the hills like a mist
it rode bareback on the wind like a Berserker
it rattled and shook
all of the farmhouse doors and all of the farmhouse windows
it even made the teacups shake on the breakfast table
like there was an earthquake going on

the noise
the constant mooing and moaning
got so incessant
that at night time
Farmer's wife and his mistress
couldn't sleep

this irritated Farmer immensely
the more time those two spent awake
the more likely it was that they'd bump into each other

so Farmer concocted an idea

he said to his wife
that he was going to give them all
the opportunity to decide for themselves

Martin Hayes

then he said to his mistress
I'll teach those fuckers
you watch

an election
that's what we need
he spluttered over his Eton mess

first he wrote a slogan on the side of a muck-spreader
telling the oxen what it *could* be like
with Farmer

then he got Laws the undertaker
to send leaflets out on social media
telling the oxen what it *would* be like
without Farmer

all of the oxen were confused

no ox dreamed for a month

when the day of the election came around
every ox stood in the rain and mud outside the slaughterhouse
waiting to vote

at 11 pm
it was announced
that Farmer had won
by a landslide

thus proving once again
that the majority of oxen
are far too scared far too safe
to listen to any kind of voice emanating from inside their guts
and would much rather have a Farmer
thwacking them into shape
than stand on their own four feet
because that makes oxen feel dizzy

Ox on Alcohol

we don't need that bloody Farmer
to feed us
keep this leaky barn roof over our heads
who does he think he is!?
putting these paltry amounts of food
in front of us?
are we supposed to be thankful
for his meagre wage packets!?
he's the one who should be thankful!

Ox took in a deep breath
wobbling a little on his legs
as all the other oxen who had been drinking
mooed and cheered out in support
stamping their hooves into the dust

I know what we should do
let's all go to Farmer's house
and wake him up!
tell him that we're not putting up with this anymore
that without us
he is nothing!
that he needs to start showing us
a bit more respect
and start giving us
more than just the crumbs
left on his table!

Hurrah! Hurrah!

all the other oxen mooed

let's go right now!

Martin Hayes

and because this seemed
like the greatest idea ever at the time
it wasn't long before all the oxen
were gathered at Farmer's door
under a moon that illuminated the whole courtyard
bone white

and just as one of the oxen
was about to put his hoof through Farmer's door
one of the oxen at the back mooed

this is not going to end well

before everything suddenly went black
like an eye shutting out the world
just before being hit by a truck

Martin Hayes

Ox with a Hangover After the Crime

it was all a bit fuzzy
but the pain in his head
the way it felt like there was a chainsaw
swinging about at the back of it
told him that it had been
a bit of a night

and the way his heart
wasn't keeping its usual
slow predictable pump
but rather thumping about missing beats
and quivering all over the place
told him that he'd drunk too much

and the sudden sweats and uncontrollable shaking
that erupted from the deepest parts of him
told him that he was getting
a little bit too old for this

and then there was the faint recollection
of doing something embarrassing
in front of the rest of the herd
that he'll always be remembered
and never forgiven for
that made him cringe and worry
what he might've done

it was only when the neon strip lighting
glinting off the steel hooks
that hung from the overhead conveyor
brought him back to his senses
did he realise that he was trussed up
hanging upside down

and when he began
slowly swinging back and forth
from the sudden movement forwards
that's when he remembered
Farmer's door
broken in two
like a terrible accident

the sudden electric jolt
coming from out of nowhere
releasing its current into him
falling to the floor on his knees
along with all of the other oxen

and the last thing he thinks he heard was

take that
you ungrateful ox
it's the abattoir for you boy!

but he couldn't be sure
as he continued slowly moving
along the line
hanging upside down
gently swinging back and forth
unsure of whether this was the end
or just the start of something else

Martin Hayes

Ox at the Gates of Heaven

*"If you prod an ox too much, they have heart attacks. If you get an ox in the chute
that's had the shit prodded out of it and he has a heart attack or refuses to move,
you take a meat hook and hook it into his bunghole. They're too big to move them
out the way like you can a pig, you have to call for a colleague and the two of you
shove a meat hook into each one of its cheeks and you drag him forward outta
the way. You've got to keep the chute clear man, no matter what."*

  – Slaughterhouse worker, Wisconsin , 2014.

and then there was the single file entry method
funnelling the herd in
to reduce the levels of stress

the white rubber wellington boots
flecked with blood
protecting the feet of a Vasily Blokhin

the silver hooks of a Torquemada
to upturn the world on its head

the white ceramic guttering of a Pol Pot's throat
accelerating the rivers of blood
into the stomach of the Earth

the burnt out Fiat smoking in the abandoned skull
of a Mussolini

the black bud of poison squeezed from the festering anus
of a Thatcher

the breathtakingly beautiful bright strobe lighting
of a Blair

the drone
of an Obama

the empty testes
of a Trump

the lullabies
of a Marine Le Pen

then God's final judgment

a bolt through the head for all

and a barcode slapped on your flank
to get you out of the gates of this Hell

Ox and Cow Under Moonlight

on an August evening after a particularly hard day pulling their ploughs
Ox and Cow wandered away from the rest of the herd
and stood at the furthest edge of the holding field
resting their chins on the hedgerow
staring up at the moon

it was quiet
and peaceful

do you know what Daisy?

no Hector what?

my old cow used to say
that the moon was once covered in buttercups

really – that's obviously an old cow's tale though
isn't it?

apparently not
apparently a long time ago
it once used to be so close to the farm
that you could see them

really?

yes
and what's more
it was that close
you could sort of leap-jump
right onto it

no way!

Martin Hayes

way!
and that's not all either Daisy
apparently the buttercups on the moon
were different to the buttercups on the farm
they used to do something funny to you
after you'd eaten them

really – what was that then?

well my old bull said that they made your insides become your outsides

oh
I bet that hurt

no
not your insides
like your stomach or your lungs
but your 'insides'

oh …
why was that then?

I don't know
but apparently they made your head go all funny
and you could see everything
through every mystery
inside every secret
even that Farmer
was really the same
as all of us cattle

WHAT?

yes I know
but best of all Daisy
is that they apparently made you feel
more than good
like … that everything …
was going to be ok

well that's just preposterous

as Daisy and Hector stood under the light of the moon
resting their chins on the hedgerow
not knowing what to believe
or exactly what it was
that was up there
which once upon a time
was enough

Martin Hayes

A Night in the Leaky Barn

this Ox and this Cow ate each other
it wasn't ordered or planned or anything
they just became bored one night
and stoked up a hell of a hunger

gradually he chewed up all of her smiles
kept them in his intestines like eggs in a nest
she delighted in teasing his words
into the microwave
where she nuked them
into seeping bulging-eyed monsters
he munched on her eyes until all she could see was the back of his throat
she steamed away his tongue for that
he filleted of her womb to get her back
she peeled back the rind of his sternum
and licked on the marrowy insides like it were an ice-lolly
he uprooted both of her legs
then sank in up to his neck – the Hyena
she just laid back and laughed louder
sucking clean the mango stone she'd found in his head
he put his hands inside her stomach
and clenched them to fists as tight as he could
she jumped up and down on his eyeballs
as though she was beating meat
he put in the oven her nails and teeth
she brought out her blender and purified his penis

he said he was full now
she said she was tired
and besides

it wasn't fun anymore
so they fell asleep
what was left fitted tightly up against what was left
and never woke up again

until morning
when the strapping into their ploughs
diverted their hunger away
from each other

Martin Hayes

Ox Witnesses Yet Another Birthing

here it comes the new born
with nothing in front of it
and everything behind it broken
who can predict what this fresh sun will instigate
its brightness is not for us but ours to devour
hot blood has already knitted the words of its poem
warming up not only its mother but other planets also
there is a depth to this deeper than known soil
it sits somewhere in darkness wearing darkness
we are resigned unknowing how it all works
no blueprints survive
we must go blind into its waters every time

Ox Gets a Visit From Social Services

they visited him once
never needed to knock
the leaky barn not being his
doors were left off latch
inside the filth afflicted
no pictures nailed the wall to yearn a lost heart
and not one but sixty of them stood
swishing their tails staring
at what the walls might bring their still beating hearts
language was not chucked around this place uselessly
every one knew only one word none of them could quell
none of them!
they were prisoners of their own song
Hunger it was called

Little Ox

Little Ox wanted to make love to Beyoncé
he wanted to wine and dine Jennifer Lawrence
take her back to his leaky barn
so that he could run the tips of strawberries
all over her body

Little Ox wanted to sit on a throne
wearing £500 limited edition trainers
with solid-silver pistols in his hooves
while bubble-butt women
shook themselves about in front of him
to the tunes of Eminem

Little Ox wanted to holiday in Thailand and St Kitts and the Maldives
he wanted to sit on a yacht
in the Bay of Biscay
drinking Cristal champagne
snorting coke
so he could post it all up on his Instagram

Little Ox wanted more
of what he was being told he wanted
he wanted to believe in and follow
everything that the Communications and Media Department of the farm
had been feeding into the leaky barn
ever since he was a calf

Little Ox wanted more and more
of what he was being told
he wanted

Martin Hayes

because little oxen do that
they need to feel
they are part of something
like a gang
or a confederacy

like a herd

so that when they grow up
to become big oxen
and stop believing in anything
at least they can say

*I used to believe in something
once*

Ox After the Tragedy

the oxen worked hard
there was no doubt about that
but there were hundreds of oxen
thousands millions billions even

there were so many oxen
that in true supply and demand fashion
none of the oxen were worth anything

you could slaughter one here
starve one to death there
squeeze one in a fist until he pops
and no one would even care

you could herd hundreds of them up into a leaky barn
so that they all had to live on top of each other
then at night time
you could set fire to the lot
and when the smoke disappears from the sky
as it always does
due to the spinning and whirring of the Earth
it is like nothing has happened

just 62 oxen less

just a burnt out leaky barn
silhouetted against a blue sky

just the cacophony
of the spinning and whirring
of the Earth

Martin Hayes

Ox Tries to Sleep

it was often difficult for Ox to shut his eyes
but when he did
the deep vast impenetrable black
was everywhere

Ox would feel around for a thought or image
to keep him company
but all there was was this blackness
sticky and absolute

and this sensation
that there was a cliff-edge near by
that would solve all his problems

Ox had to open up his eyes again
it was just too terrifying
like getting lost in the thickest part of a wood
with no moonlight able to get through the canopy
like finding yourself swallowed up into the stomach of yourself
before realising
you were in the deepest part of the ocean
or having a blanket wrapped around your head
with a farmer's knee shoved into the nape of your neck
twisting and pulling it tighter
until something gave in
or snapped

there was no choice though
Ox had to face the black
if he was going to sleep

so Ox took in a deep breath
and closed his eyes again

the black descended almost immediately
the fear and panic rose
but he held on grinding his teeth
until he found that cliff-edge –
or it found him?
it's hard to say exactly how it happens –
and fell off its edge

and as Ox was falling
he suddenly realised that this blackness
the fears inside him
that was him
that was what
he was made of

Martin Hayes

Ox Dealing with the Light

when light comes in through the cracks in the leaky barn
it hurt Ox's eyes

when light reflects off the steel handle of Farmer's thwacking stick
Ox's flanks quiver and tremble

when the low morning light of the sun
reflects off the puddles in the yard
Ox's heart sinks

when moonlight
bathes the dusty roots with its magic
Ox tosses and turns
thinking that a great spell is being placed upon him

and when the lights of the abattoir
burn through the night from a distance
looking like a search party
coming to the rescue
Ox hasn't a clue
that is where it will all end

which all helps go to prove
when you see an ox
momentarily pause in a field
swishing his head from side to side
like in a great struggle to set something free
there's no need to worry
about the revolution starting anytime soon
because all it is
is Ox pretending again
that he's got something going on up there
when really there is only blackness and fog
and the pain from all of this light

Ox and the Tractor's Legacy

after Ox had not been laced up into a plough for more than six months
because the tractors were now doing all of his work
four times more efficiently
at half the cost

after all the food had dried up
and water
had become stale as an old memory

after the darkness beneath his eyelids
had become like a shutdown theatre
clinging to the end of a pier
in which the wooden Punch
couldn't find his pulsating Judy

and after the pain in his head
had become a constant throb
like an invisible audience
laughing at all of his errors

Ox realised
that his position in the leaky barn
had become untenable

so Ox started looking around
to see if he could find another way
of being an ox

the options didn't look promising though

call centre operator – not the best telephone manner – unable to pick up a phone

waiter – too much hunger – the food would never get to the table courier – bad sense of direction – would have to lay down 15 minutes every time before it rained

dustman – all that muck to rummage through – all those leftovers to eat

telesales – the moos – the confusion

there was nothing left for Ox to do
other than to gain as much momentum as possible
and not stop
even when the edge of the cliff came up
even when the train was almost upon him
even when he sat at the kitchen table
stroking the glint of steel under moonlight
even when
being an ox
had become so overwhelmingly impossible
that all there seemed to be
was this one last final chance of escape

Ox Maybe Discovers Unicorns

Ox loved the fields
they gave him meaning
when all the leaky barn did
was pile hour upon hour of proof
that all he is
is an ox

the fields allowed Ox to stretch out his loins
use his bulk
to heave and heave
test himself
amongst other oxen

it was like a great big game
Ox knew that
but coming first was so important
so indecipherable
like discovering a very important message
inside the lining of your guts
when all the leaky barn did
was reveal everything that had already been discovered
before

there was an urgency for Ox
to find a different answer

having ruled out Redheads Rebellion and Escape
Dreams and Hope had become his favourites
the two Unicorns
he'd chosen to ride him around the graveyard's walls
into the field beyond where no one dies

Martin Hayes

it is a hard thing to do
find Unicorns
you have to start believing in them first
before they even start to appear

Ox didn't have a clue if Unicorns existed or not
he just
wished it

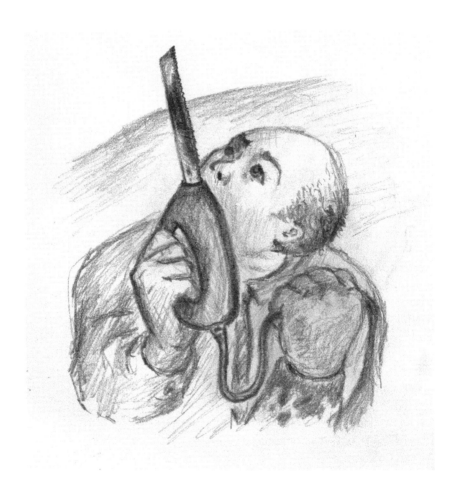

Ox Gets Dismembered

Farmer had had enough
the money wasn't coming in fast enough
the corporation tax the electricity bills
the upkeep of the thwacking sticks
having to replace them
with newer and more gruesome models
and all of thoese bloody oxen to feed
it was enough to drive Farmer to drink

whisky was his tipple
and one night
after a bottle
he decided to take it out on an ox

the next morning
when the sun started spreading its undeniable evidence across the yard
Crow couldn't believe her luck
there were the flanks of an ox
and flesh turned inside out
hung up on the line
like washing

on a pole
usually used to fly the Union Jack
an oxen's head sat

Crow cawed out in merriment
as she attached herself to it
dug in at its eyes
came back umpteen times
till her whole head blood-covered was inside its sockets
tearing away at its brains

Martin Hayes

underneath
where the vermin gather and scratch
rats and a fox or two
licked at the puddles of blood

it was a sorry sight

but nothing that couldn't be cured
by a decent lay in
a strong cup of tea
and the satisfaction
of having nothing able to stop
anything that Farmer wanted to do
at all

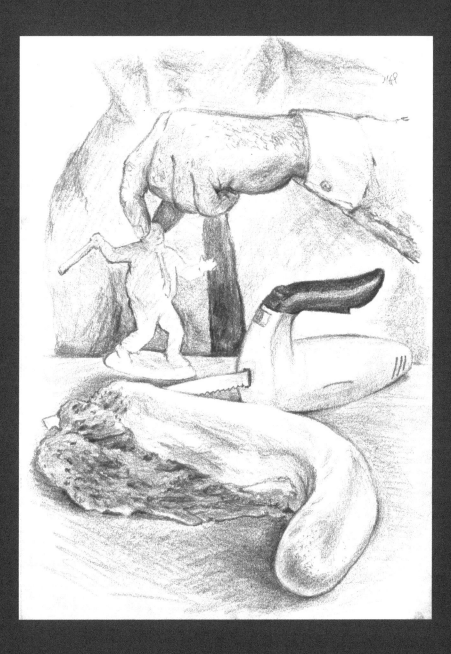

Martin Hayes

Ox's Flesh Hung Out to Dry

Crow was full on Ox's flesh
she had been feeding all morning on the atrocity

didn't even think of the events the night before
the way Farmer had stormed into the leaky barn
his blood cocked by a full bottle of whisky
randomly picking out an ox
pulling it by its horns
into a quiet corner bathed only by a strip of light
and a plug socket

firing up the 150W electric carving knife double-bladed
he felt hysterical

this feels good!

he thought to himself

setting it to work at its hips first
then its knee-joints
laughing at the way it all collapsed

the high-pitched moos were just an annoyance
it wasn't like anyone could hear
or would do anything about it
even if they could

so he spun around like a Jedi
lopping off both of its ears

he held its tail far out with one hand
before slicing it off at the root with the other

he dug and jabbed it in at both of its eyes
cleaning the sockets out with the scoops of his fingers

he opened up its back
along the spine
like a long tare along the wrapping paper
of an extremely big present

then as it lay there on its side
he rammed it into its chest
running it down almost to his balls
until everything that Ox was on the inside
was now on the outside

Farmer was exhausted
sitting there
amongst the gigantic liver
heart guts bits of eye
all of the blood and splintered bone
he just wanted to lay down
and go to sleep amongst it all

but there was the cleaning up to do!

after hosing down the scene
sweeping up all the bits and bobs
he hung what was left of Ox
out on the washing line

then hangover-driven he broke down
cried like a new-born on his knees
covered in blood

and after the sun
had crossed the sky
yet again
the yard turned to black
like the end of a very long
and disturbing play

Martin Hayes

Ox Guts

of course the oxen didn't have to go to work
it wasn't as though it was written in the trails of stars
on the bottom of the sea
or underneath the petals of a buttercup

if they could've found another way to put food on the table
keep a leaky barn roof over their heads
then they would've done it
but no matter how hard they thought
no matter how many oxen huddled together
brain-storming –
well – brain-showering you'd be better off calling it
they couldn't come up with
one single alternative

one of the oxen suddenly said

I know
maybe it is one of those things
that never happens
until you actually do it
like climbing a mountain
or knitting a hat

all of the oxen looked at each other
and let out low moos

since you had the idea
I think you should have the honour
of trying it first

the let-out-low-moos said

the next day when Farmer came to let the oxen out into the yard
so they could all be sorted
and strapped into their ploughs
the ox who'd had the idea first
refused to move

it just stood there
on the spot
waiting willing
for it to happen

Farmer thought that the ox was just being obstinate
so he thwacked it with his thwacking stick
and kicked it with his boot
but still the ox refused to move
closed its eyes and waited willing for it
to happen

Farmer
not knowing that this ox was standing up for all oxen
thinking that it was just being stubborn
pulled at its ears
and pushed his thumbs into its eyes

the ox ground its teeth
and mooed out in pain

all the other oxen out in the yard
heard the thwacks of Farmer's thwacking stick
the moos of their comrades suffering
but they didn't run to help
they didn't throw down their ploughs
and storm the leaky barn
they just waited willing for whatever it was
to happen
because this was their last chance
their only hope
lay with this ox
who'd had this idea

Martin Hayes

then all of a sudden
the sky opened up
and to the sound of trumpets and drums
there descended from the sky
the shiniest new barn you could ever wish to see
followed by the biggest pile of food
ever seen by Ox or Farmer
both of which came gently to rest
in the holding field behind the farmhouse

thus proving
once again
that miracles can happen
but only if you are lucky enough to be around an ox
who has guts

Martin Hayes

Martin Hayes

Ox and the Song of the Strong

Ox knew that he was strong
stronger than the mountains?
stronger than Elephant?
not 'arf!

he knew that the universe was unraveling
untethering itself
that the rivers were pouring themselves
into the centre of a plastic Earth
that would soon leave everything behind
dust and memory

he knew he had strength though
that he could pull all of the stars back into place
push all of the oak trees back into the sky
lift all of the oxen up off their knees
he knew
that his blood was thick with stamina
that it was made up of all the blood that had ever been before
and would ever come again

and this is what enabled Ox to sing

because after everything had been and gone
it was only blood and strength
and the songs
that would remain of him

Lightning Source UK Ltd.
Milton Keynes UK
UKHW021158140321
380293UK00006B/45